DATE DUE

APR 6 1981 *ShustaAPR* 1 7 2002			
FT. JO D 3 = 2 2 '82			
MACDO A 4 9 '84			
MACDO A- 1 27 '86			
MONTA C 3 17 '87			
JAN 2 1 1988 *Sites*			
MONTA A 1 25 '89			
APR 2 4 1998 APR 0 7 1999			
APR 0 7 1999			
APR 1 8 2000			
APR 2 4 5 2001			
MAR 2 6 2002			
APR 1 0 2002			

GAYLORD | | | PRINTED IN U.S.A.

Things to Make and Do for
EASTER

THIS BOOK IS FOR JOHN, DANA AND WENDY

Things to Make and Do for
EASTER

by Marion Cole and Olivia H. H. Cole

pictures by Olivia H. H. Cole

A Things to Make and Do Book

Franklin Watts
New York | London | 1979

Library of Congress Cataloging in Publication Data

Cole, Marion.
    Things to make and do for Easter.

    (A things to make and do book)
    SUMMARY: Includes recipes, puzzles, riddles,
games, and instructions for making Easter eggs and an
Easter basket.
    1. Easter eggs—Juvenile literature.
2. Games—Juvenile literature. 3. Riddles—
Juvenile literature. 4. Easter—Juvenile literature.
[1. Easter decorations. 2. Games. 3. Riddles.
4. Handicraft] I. Cole, Olivia H. H., joint author.
TT896.7.C65   745.59′41   78-12457
ISBN 0-531-01463-0

WHEN IS EASTER?

Easter is always on Sunday.
But which Sunday?
You can look at a calendar each year
to find out. But it is more fun to
watch the spring sky. Here's how.
March 21 is the first day of spring.
After March 21, watch the moon
each night. When you see a full
moon, Easter will be the next
Sunday.

EASTER EGGS

What you need:

Eggs
A pot with a lid
Water

What you do:

1. Put the eggs in the pot.
2. Cover with cold water. Be sure the pot handle is turned toward the back of the stove.
3. Ask a grown-up to turn on the burner for you.
4. Bring water to a bubbling boil.
5. Turn off the burner and take the pot off the heat. Ask a grown-up to help.
6. Put the lid on the pot.
7. Let the pot stand for 25 minutes.
8. Pour off water.
9. Run cold water over eggs to cool them.

It's fun to dye eggs

What you need:

    Four cups
    Measuring cup
    Boiling water (please ask a grown-up to
       help)
    Teaspoon
    Vinegar
    Yellow, red, blue, green food dyes
    Large spoon
    Hard-boiled eggs
    Paper towel
    Also: Tinted papers, pencils, Magic Markers,
       crayons, glue, buttons, yarn or wool, bits
       of lace and ribbon

What you do:

1. Half-fill each cup with boiling water.
2. Add 1 teaspoon vinegar to each cup.
3. Put 20 drops of a different food dye in each cup. Stir.
4. With the large spoon, put 1 egg in each cup. Let stand until it is the shade you want.
5. Remove egg from cup and place on paper towel to dry.
6. Glue papers, buttons, ribbons on eggs, or use Magic Markers or crayons to make designs.

Here are some ideas. Make
up your own.

THE EGG HUNT

JOHN　　**DOG**　　**PEGGY**　　**PRIZE**

had a　named Spot.　Spot loved 2

chew　and　but most of all he loved 2

chew　.　Easter morning　climbed out of

.　He put on his **RED** striped　and

BROWN　and went **DOWN**　.

"Happy Easter!" said his　and his　.

"Guess what," said his  . "Your friend

is having an Easter 🥚 hunt at her 🏠 today.

She will have 🍦 and 🌸 . Do you want **2**

go?" **"YES"** said 👦 , "can my 🐕

Spot go **2** ?" **"YES,"** said his 👩 ,

"but make sure he *does not* chew any 👟 ."

👦 called his 🐕 and went **2** 👧 's

🏠 . Each of the 👨‍👩‍👧 was given an

Easter 🧺 and told to hunt for 🥚 .

The  or 👧 who found the **RED** 🥚 would win a 🎁. TEDDY found an 🥚 under a 🪑. ROSA found an 🥚 behind the 🚪. Every **1** found an 🥚 but 👦. He was **SAD**. Suddenly 👦 🪚 his 🐕 chewing on an old 👟. **"STOP"** said 👦, and took the 👟 away from his Spot. The **RED** 🥚 rolled out of the 👟 into 👦's ✋. 👧's

gave the . 's

Spot got a **BIG** with a

RED on it. The end.

You can have an egg hunt like Peggy's

What you need:

Lots of hard-boiled, dyed eggs.
One egg that is special — the only one that
is red, or blue, or whatever you choose.

How to play:

1. Hide the eggs.
2. Tell everyone what the special egg looks
   like.
3. Tell your family or friends when to start
   looking for the eggs.

The person who finds the special
egg wins.
The person who finds the most eggs
comes in second.

AN EASTER STORY

Long ago in a faraway country lived a poor old woman. She loved children and welcomed them to her home. Poor as she was, she planned treats and surprises for them. But one year when Easter came, the old woman had no money at all. She did have plenty of eggs and a happy thought. She dyed the eggs to match every hue of the rainbow and hid them in little nests which she made of sticks and grass.

When the children came, the old woman said: "Your Easter surprises are in the garden. See if you can find them."

The children looked and looked. Then, just as they found the eggs, a rabbit hopped out of one of the nests. The children were delighted. "Oh look," they cried. "The rabbit left pretty eggs for our Easter surprise!"

RABBIT FOOD?

It's a healthful Bunny Salad!

Make *two*—one for yourself and one for your friend.

What you need:

1 small can of pears
4 lettuce leaves
2 blanched almonds for each bunny
2 raisins or whole cloves for each bunny
1 maraschino cherry
½ cup (114 ml) of shredded coconut

What you do:

1. Tear the lettuce in shreds and on two small plates make lettuce nests

2. Place half a pear (round side up) in each nest.

3. Now you create your bunnies! Use blanched almonds for the ears, raisins or whole cloves for the eyes, a bit of maraschino cherry for the pink noses.

4. A little pile of coconut will make lovely cotton tails.

You now have two delicious Bunny Salads. If you like, you can serve them with French dressing or mayonnaise.

THE SHOE RABBIT

There once was a rabbit who lived in a shoe. Having nothing to do, he hid his eight Easter eggs around his house and then could not remember where he put them. Can you help him fill his basket?

(Answer on page 47)

19

You can make an
EASTER BASKET

What you need:

An egg box
A strip of cardboard
Scissors
Four pipe cleaners
Paint, crayons, bits of paper, yarn, and
   ribbon

What you do:

1. Cut the top off the egg box.
2. Cut a handle from the cardboard.
3. Put a hole through the handle and egg box (as shown). Do this on both sides.
4. Put two pipe cleaners through each hole (as shown).
5. Tie.
6. Make your basket pretty by painting.
7. If you wish, you can fill your basket with flowers or eggs or jelly beans.

SILLY BUNNY'S PARTY

Silly Billy Bunny is giving an Easter party but he has mixed up his holidays. Can you find the six things he has done wrong?

(Answer on page 47)

23

A SPRING STORY
WITHOUT WORDS

SPRING GARDEN

Now is the time to grow an indoor garden!

What you need:

> The top 1 inch (2.5 cm) of a carrot
> A shallow dish
> Water

What you do:

1. Place the carrot in the shallow dish and add water.
2. Check the carrot every day to see that the stump is wet.

Soon your carrot stump will have lovely lacy leaves — a pretty plant for your room.

What you need:

> Grapefruit, orange, or lemon seeds
> Soil
> Small foil containers

What you do:

1. Fill containers with soil.
2. Plant 12 seeds in each one.
3. Water the soil well.
4. Place the container in a warm, light spot.
5. Check them every day. As the soil dries, add more water.

Be patient and in four to six weeks your containers will be filled with small plants with shiny green leaves.

BUTTON BUTTERCUPS

While you are waiting for your seeds to sprout, you may want to make your own flowers.

What you need:

> Six buttons
> Six pipe cleaners
> Stiff construction paper

What you do:

1. Cut out your flower from the construction paper.
2. Choose a button to go with your flower.
3. Stick the tip of one pipe cleaner up through your flower, through one hole in the button, down through another hole, and back down through the flower.
4. Twist the short tip of the pipe cleaner around the long end, under the flower and button. The long end of the pipe cleaner is the flower's stem.

You can add these flowers to the plants in your foil containers, or you can make a bouquet of them, or use them for decorations on the Easter dinner table.

28

My Easter eggs
grew little legs
and walked away
on Easter day.

29

HERE COMES PETER COTTONTAIL
—just in time for Easter!

What you need:

One piece of stiff white construction paper
Crayons
Cotton
Paste
Scissors

3. DO NOT CUT FOLD.

CUT

PASTE

4.

5.

What you do:

1. Fold the construction paper in half.
2. Draw *half* a bunny shape (as shown), using the folded line as the middle.
3. Cut out the bunny (as shown).
4. Draw face and whiskers on one side.
5. Paste the cotton tail on the other side.

BUNNY MAGIC
(and other optical illusions)

The Magic Bunny has a few tricks up his sleeve. He plays tricks with your eyes.

Can you make Bunny's goldfish kiss?

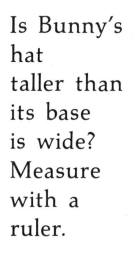

Is Bunny's hat taller than its base is wide? Measure with a ruler.

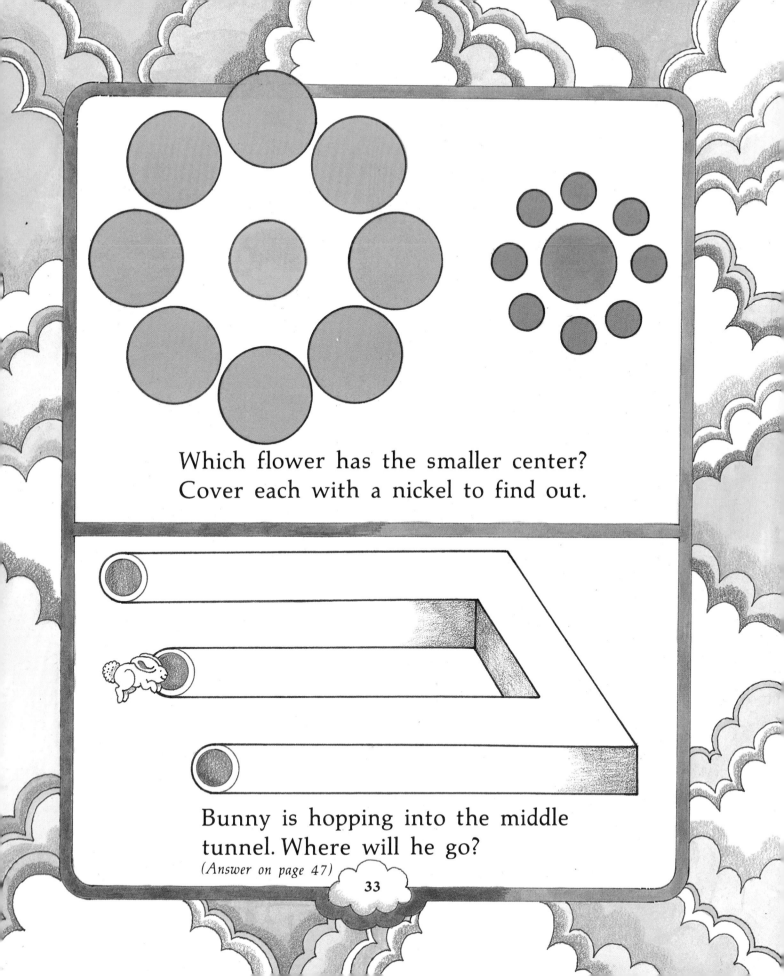

Which flower has the smaller center?
Cover each with a nickel to find out.

Bunny is hopping into the middle
tunnel. Where will he go?

(Answer on page 47)

33

FIND BUDDY BUNNY

Betty Bunny's babies all look alike except for Buddy Bunny. Can you help Betty Bunny find Buddy?

(Answer on page 47)

BUNNY LANGUAGE

Benny and Bonnie Bunny are talking. Do U no what they are saying?

(Answer on page 48)

"G U R A Q T."

"I N V U."

"2 Ys U R
2 Ys U B
I C U R
2 Ys 4 me !"

35

37

AN EASTER EGG RACE
how to win by a nose!

What you need:

Tape or chalk
A hard-boiled Easter egg for each player

How to play:

1. Mark a "Start" and "Finish" line with tape or chalk.
2. Give an egg to each player.
3. Line up players at the "Start" line.
4. Tell each player to roll the egg from the "Start" line to the "Finish" line, touching the egg only with his or her nose.
5. Yell, "Go!"

The player who pushes his or her egg across the "Finish" line first wins the race.

WORD MIX-UP

What you do:

1. Look at the pictures.
2. Fix the letters so they spell the word that names the picture.
3. Keep the answers in order.
4. Write the first letter of each answer.

You will have the name of an Easter friend.

(Answer on page 48)

S	R	E	O	＝
P	P	E	A	L	＝
E	B	E	＝
D	B	I	R	＝
N	K	I	＝
E	R	T	E	＝

40

Betty and Bobby Bunny are baking an Easter cake. There are six things on their table they do not need. Can you find them?

(Answer on page 48)

BETTY AND BOBBY BUNNY BAKE

41

MAKE YOUR OWN MOSAICS

What you need:

> The eggshells you peeled from your dyed
>   Easter eggs
> Plastic bag
> Lightweight cardboard
> Glue

What you do:

1. Put the eggshells in the plastic bag and crush them with your hands, being careful not to make the pieces too small.
2. Spread glue over part of the cardboard (only a small area because the glue will dry quickly) and press the eggshells, dyed side up, into the glue.
3. Spread more glue and repeat with eggshells. You can make a pretty design, or you may want to make an object, such as a fish or an animal.
4. Repeat with glue and shells until your work of art is complete.

Here are some ideas.

43

EASTER HATS

Everyone bought new Easter hats for the Easter parade but the wind has blown them into the air. Can you tell who owns each hat?

(Answer on page 48)

44

BE A DETECTIVE!

Who made each set of footprints?

Follow the prints to learn who found the Easter basket!

(Answer on page 48)

46

Answers to the puzzle on pages 18 and 19:

Answers to the puzzle on pages 22 and 23:
Look for:
   A firecracker
   A jack-o'-lantern
   A valentine
   A Christmas tree
   George Washington's Birthday cake
   Pilgrims and their turkey

Answers to the puzzles on pages 32 and 33:
Stare hard between the goldfish and move the page slowly toward you.

The hat is as high as it is wide.

The circles are the same size.

Bunny will go nowhere. It is not a tunnel.

Answer to the puzzle on page 34:
Buddy Bunny has no eyebrows.

Answers to the puzzle on page 35:
"Gee, you are a cutie."
"I envy you."

"Too wise you are
Too wise you be.
I see you are
too wise for me!"

Answers to the puzzle on page 40:
Rose
Apple
Bee
Bird
Ink
Tree

Answers to the puzzle on page 41:
Look for:
   A key
   A letter
   A saw
   A rose
   A shoe
   A baseball

Answers to the puzzle on pages 44 and 45:

Answer to the puzzle on page 46:
The little girl found the Easter basket.